W9-ASL-419

DATE DUE

Thurgood Marshall

A Photo-Illustrated Biography

by Karen Bush Gibson

Consultant:
Kathy Shurtleff
Assistant Director
Supreme Court Historical Society

Bridgestone Books
an imprint of Capstone Press
Mankato, Minnesota

Bridgestone Books are published by Capstone Press
151 Good Counsel Drive, P.O. Box 669, Mankato, Minnesota 56002
http://www.capstone-press.com

Library of Congress Cataloging-in-Publication Data
Gibson, Karen Bush.
   Thurgood Marshall: a photo-illustrated biography/by Karen Bush Gibson.
   p. cm.—(Photo-illustrated biographies)
   Includes bibliographical references and index.
   Summary: A biography of the civil rights lawyer who helped end school segregation
and served as a Supreme Court Justice.
   ISBN 0-7368-1113-3
   1. Marshall, Thurgood, 1908–1993—Juvenile literature. 2. United States. Supreme
Court—Biography—Juvenile literature. 3. African American judges—Biography—Juvenile
literature. [1. Marshall, Thurgood, 1908–1993. 2. Lawyers. 3. Judges. 4. African Americans—
Biography.] I. Title. II. Series.
KF8745.M34 G53 2002
347.73'2634—dc21   2001005406

Editorial Credits
Gillia Olson, editor; Karen Risch, product planning editor; Timothy Halldin, cover
   designer; Steve Christensen, interior layout designer; Alta Schaffer, photo researcher

Photo Credits
Antonio Tobias Mendez, Thurgood Marshall, Annapolis MD. Courtesy Maryland Commission
   on Artistic Property of the Maryland State Archives, MSA SC 1545-2944, 20
AP/Wide World Photos, 16
Bettmann/CORBIS, 4, 18
CORBIS, 6, 10
Library of Congress, 12, 14
Lincoln University Archives, Langston Hughes Memorial Library, 8
Stock Montage, Inc., cover
1 2 3 4 5 6 07 06 05 04 03 02

Table of Contents

"Equal means getting the same thing, at the same time, and in the same place."
–Thurgood, during arguments for *Brown versus the Board of Education*, 1954

Civil Rights Champion

Thurgood Marshall fought for African Americans' civil rights. These rights promise freedom and equal treatment under the law.

African Americans and whites were segregated when Thurgood was young. Laws separated African-American and white children in schools. Laws also separated African Americans and whites in theaters, restaurants, and other public places. African Americans and whites were supposed to have separate but equal treatment.

But African Americans did not receive equal treatment. Schools for African Americans were not as good as white schools. African Americans often were forced to sit in the worst seats in public places.

Thurgood worked as a lawyer to change these unfair laws. He also was the first African-American justice to serve on the U.S. Supreme Court.

Thurgood was the first African American to serve on the U.S. Supreme Court.

"We will see that the true miracle was not the birth of the Constitution, but its life…"
–Thurgood, during a speech, May 6, 1987

Childhood

Thurgood was born in Baltimore, Maryland, on July 2, 1908. Thurgood's father, William, worked as a train porter and later at a country club. His mother, Norma, was a teacher. Thurgood had an older brother named William Aubrey.

Thurgood liked to play jokes at school. The school principal made Thurgood memorize the U.S. Constitution when he got into trouble. The Constitution explains the U.S. system of laws and government. Thurgood asked questions about the 13th, 14th, and 15th amendments. These amendments promised people equal rights. Thurgood saw that African Americans were not treated the way the law promised.

Thurgood often debated with his father and brother at the dinner table. They argued different sides to many topics. Thurgood learned how to use reason to win arguments.

This photograph shows how Baltimore looked in the early 1900s when Thurgood was born.

College

Thurgood graduated from Frederick Douglass High School in Baltimore at age 16. He began studying at Lincoln University in 1925. Lincoln was a college in Pennsylvania for African-American students.

Thurgood joined the debate club after entering college. He discovered that he enjoyed debating. It reminded him of the many talks he had with his father. Thurgood also remembered the Constitution's promise of equal rights. He decided to become a lawyer.

During college, Thurgood met Vivian Burey. Her friends called her Buster. Thurgood and Buster got married during his last year of college in 1929.

Thurgood applied to the University of Maryland Law School. He was denied admission because of his race. He decided to go to Howard Law School in Washington, D.C.

This photo of Thurgood (second row, second from right) was taken at Lincoln University in 1926.

Practicing Law

Thurgood graduated first in his class at Howard Law School in 1933. After he graduated, Thurgood started his own law practice in Baltimore.

Thurgood worked on many cases. But his favorites were equal rights cases. Many people with equal rights cases did not have money to pay a lawyer. Thurgood would take jobs for free. People called him "the freebie lawyer."

In 1934, Thurgood began working for the National Association for the Advancement of Colored People (NAACP) in Baltimore. The NAACP defends African Americans' civil rights.

In 1938, Thurgood closed his practice. He became a full-time lawyer for the NAACP. Thurgood helped change laws that made it hard for African Americans to vote. He made it easier for African-American soldiers to use their education benefits after World War II (1939–1945).

Thurgood often held practice trials before trying civil rights cases.

"Segregation of Negroes...brands the Negro with the mark of inferiority and asserts that he's not fit to associate with white people."
–Thurgood, during arguments for *Brown versus the Board of Education*, 1954

School Segregation

Some of Thurgood's cases went to the U.S. Supreme Court. This court is the highest court in the United States. Thurgood won 29 of 32 cases that went to the Supreme Court. People began to call him "Mr. Civil Rights."

Thurgood worked on many cases about school segregation. In 1954, he argued a case called *Brown versus the Board of Education*. In this case, some African-American students tried to enroll in white schools. The white schools were close to their homes. The African-American schools were far from their homes. Officials would not let the African-American students attend the white schools.

Thurgood showed that segregation made African-American children feel that whites were better than they were. Thurgood won the case. This decision made school segregation against the law.

Thurgood is shown smiling (center) after winning *Brown versus the Board of Education*.

Changes

In 1955, Thurgood faced changes in his personal life. Buster was diagnosed with cancer. Thurgood stopped working so he could care for Buster. But she died that year. She and Thurgood had been married for 25 years.

Thurgood married Cecilia Suyat almost a year later. He called her Cissy. They worked together for the NAACP. Cissy was a secretary. Thurgood and Cissy had two sons, Thurgood Jr. and John William. Thurgood enjoyed spending time with his sons.

Thurgood continued to gain people's respect for his civil rights efforts. In 1961, Thurgood went to the African nation of Kenya. He helped leaders there write a new constitution. In Kenya, Thurgood helped protect white people's civil rights. Whites were the minority in Kenya.

This photo shows Thurgood with his wife Cecilia and sons John (left) and Thurgood Jr.

Judge and Justice

On September 23, 1961, President John Kennedy chose Thurgood to be a judge on the U.S. Court of Appeals for the Second Circuit. Thurgood was one of the first African-American federal judges. As an appeals judge, Thurgood heard cases from lower courts. People could appeal decisions they thought were wrong. They then could take their cases to the Supreme Court.

In 1964, President Lyndon Johnson chose Thurgood to be solicitor general. This person represents the U.S. government in legal matters. In this job, Thurgood won 14 out of 19 cases in front of the Supreme Court.

In 1967, an opening came up on the Supreme Court. The nine justices on the Supreme Court decide cases by majority vote. President Johnson chose Thurgood. On October 2, 1967, he became the first African-American Supreme Court justice.

President Lyndon Johnson shook Thurgood's hand after Thurgood became solicitor general.

"What is striking is the role legal principles have played throughout America's history in determining the condition of Negroes. They were enslaved by law, emancipated by law, disenfranchised and segregated by law, and, finally, they have begun to win equality by law."
–Thurgood, during a speech, May 6, 1987

A Voice for Rights

Thurgood wanted all people to be treated equally. He stood up for the rights of African Americans, American Indians, women, and the poor. Thurgood also tried to stop discrimination. Discrimination is when people make unfair decisions about others because of their race, gender, or nation of birth.

In the 1970s and 1980s, segregation still was a problem. Whites and African Americans often still lived in separate neighborhoods. Neighborhood schools then were segregated. Thurgood worked hard to find ways to integrate schools and neighborhoods. He believed whites and African Americans should live and attend schools together.

Thurgood wanted to protect all constitutional rights. Many Supreme Court cases were about the First Amendment. This amendment promises that people can speak freely about their opinions.

Thurgood became the first African-American Supreme Court justice in 1967.

Later Years

By the 1980s, several Supreme Court justices had retired. The judges that replaced them often did not feel the same way about equal rights as Thurgood did. He was afraid that the United States would lose ground in the fight for equal rights.

Thurgood sometimes disagreed with the Supreme Court's majority opinion. He sometimes wrote dissenting opinions to show people that he disagreed with a decision. He argued when he believed people's rights were in danger.

Thurgood once said he would serve on the Supreme Court until he was 110. But health problems forced him to retire in 1991.

Thurgood died on January 24, 1993, at the age of 84. People remember him as a great lawyer and a great justice. His efforts led to more equality for people of all races.

This statue at the University of Maryland honors Thurgood's work for civil rights.

Fast Facts about Thurgood Marshall

 Thurgood's real name was Thoroughgood, after his grandfather. He shortened it in second grade.

 During college, Thurgood and his friends integrated a nearby theater by sitting in the "whites only" section.

 Thurgood worked so hard on his cases that he was hospitalized in 1941 for exhaustion.

Dates in Thurgood Marshall's Life

1908—Born July 2 in Baltimore, Maryland

1929—Marries Vivian "Buster" Burey

1933—Graduates from Howard Law School and starts a law practice

1934—Begins working for the NAACP

1954—Wins *Brown versus the Board of Education*

1955—Marries Cecilia "Cissy" Suyat

1961—Chosen as judge on U.S. Court of Appeals for the Second Circuit

1964—Named U.S. solicitor general by President Johnson

1967—Becomes first African-American justice of the U.S. Supreme Court

1991—Retires from the Supreme Court

1993—Dies on January 24 in Bethesda, Maryland

Words to Know

civil rights (SIV-il RITES)—people's rights to freedom and equal treatment under the law

court of appeals (KORT UHV uh-PEELS)—a court that hears cases from lower courts

discrimination (diss-krim-i-NAY-shuhn)—treating people unfairly because of their race, country of birth, or gender

dissenting opinion (di-SENT-ing uh-PIN-yuhn)—the views of the judges who do not vote with the majority in a case

enroll (en-ROLL)—to sign up to attend a school

integrate (IN-tuh-grate)—to include people of all races

porter (POR-tur)—a person who carries luggage and calls out train stops for passengers

segregate (SEG-ruh-gate)—to separate or keep people apart from the main group

Read More

Dunham, Montrew. *Thurgood Marshall: Young Justice.* Childhood of Famous Americans. New York: Aladdin Paperbacks, 1998.

Kent, Deborah. *Thurgood Marshall and the Supreme Court.* Cornerstones of Freedom. New York: Children's Press, 1997.

Williams, Carla. *Thurgood Marshall.* Journey to Freedom. Chanhassen, Minn.: Child's World, 2002.

Useful Addresses

Brown v. Board of Education National Historic Site
424 South Kansas Avenue
Suite 220
Topeka, KS 66603-3441

The National Civil Rights Museum
450 Mulberry Street
Memphis, TN 38103-4214

Internet Sites

Brown v. Board of Education National Historic Site
http://www.nps.gov/brvb
Civil Rights Law and History
http://www.usdoj.gov/kidspage/crt/crtmenu.htm

Index